为什么树叶掉了

Sharing the Planet | Non-Fiction Series

Copyright © 2022 by Level Learning, INC. and Washington Yu Ying PCS™
Original and Edited Text Copyright © 2022 by Washington Yu Ying PCS™

All rights reserved. No part of this book in whole or part may be reproduced without written permission from the publisher.

Published by Level Learning, INC.

Content Contributors:
Washington Yu Ying PCS™ - Qianyi (Shirley) Zhang, Pearl Zao He You
Level Learning - Jingyao Qi

Illustrations by: Matt Austin, Josh Taira

Leveling classification based on Level Learning standard.
For full description, visit www.levellearning.com

ISBN 978-1-64040-055-9
Simplified Chinese Edition

About Level Learning:

Level Learning provides a literacy focused curriculum specifically designed for K-12 Chinese as a Second Language classrooms. Our program offers 20 levels of specific and detailed objectives, leveled texts and passages, mastery-based online assessment, and analytics to enable data-driven instruction. Level Learning reading curriculum for both literature and informational text emphasize grammar and comprehension skills to help teachers develop confident and independent Chinese language readers. The non-fiction series of books are specifically designed to support our informational text course based on multiple national standards. To learn more about our entire offering, visit www.levellearning.com.

About Washington Yu Ying PCS™:

Washington Yu Ying PCS is a Mandarin English dual language immersion International Baccalaureate (IB) World school. Yu Ying's mission is to inspire and prepare young people to create a better world by challenging them to reach their full potential in a nurturing Chinese/English educational environment. Yu Ying's comprehensive IB, dual immersion curriculum equips students with global competencies for success in the real world. As a leader in immersion education, Yu Ying is determined to advance Chinese language programs and global citizenry education by helping other schools create and strengthen their Chinese programs. For more information, email: products@washingtonyuying.org

树木的生长离不开阳光、空气和水。阳光、空气和水是怎么帮助树木生长的呢？

和动物一样,树木也需要呼吸。树根会吸收水,然后把水输送到树叶上。树叶也会从空气中吸收水分。

树叶把水、阳光和空气变成营养。

树叶再把营养输送给树干。树木就是这样生长的。

秋天到了。天气开始变冷,阳光和水也开始变少。

没有足够的水和阳光,树木需要的营养就不够了。

树木会死掉吗？当然不会。树木会在内部切断和树叶的联系。树叶就会慢慢变黄、变干。

没多久,树叶就掉下来了。

这样，树木可以生存下来。第二年春天，树木会长出新的叶子。

Glossary

	Pinyin	English Definition
生长	shēng zhǎng	growth
离不开	lí bu kāi	inseparable
阳光	yáng guāng	sunshine
空气	kōng qì	air
需要	xū yào	need
呼吸	hū xī	to breathe
输送	shū sòng	to transport
树叶	shù yè	leaf
变	biàn	to change
营养	yíng yǎng	nutrition
树干	shù gàn	tree trunk
秋天	qiū tiān	autumn
开始	kāi shǐ	start
冷	lěng	cold
少	shǎo	less

	Pinyin	English Definition
足够	zú gòu	enough
不够	bú gòu	not enough
内部	nèi bù	inside
切断	qiē duàn	to cut off
联系	lián xì	link
干	gān	dry
掉	diào	fall
生存	shēng cún	to survive

www.ingramcontent.com/pod-product-compliance
Lightning Source LLC
Chambersburg PA
CBHW041222070526
44584CB00001B/49